Railways of the
NORTH EASTERN REGION
in the Latter Days of Steam

Malcolm Castledine

BOOK LAW PUBLICATIONS

ISBN 1 901945 41 3

DEDICATION

To the memory of my good friend, the late Peter Edgington, to whom all things North Eastern meant everything. Many a Tuesday afternoon we shunted colliery yards, sent thousands of tons of iron ore (in 56-ton bogie hoppers with Q6's, Q7's and 9F's) up to Consett, and ran numerous special passenger trains with B16's, etc. All in 4mm scale of course.

First published in the United Kingdom
by Book Law Publications
382 Carlton Hill, Nottingham, NG4 1JA
Printed and bound by The Amadeus Press, Cleckheaton, West Yorkshire

INTRODUCTION

The Nottingham branch of the RCTS were instrumental in giving me my first taste of North Eastern Region steam which came about during a railtour to Darlington works and shed in May 1962. However, it was my Geography master at school who got me to join the RCTS in the first place and therefore must take responsibility for introducing me to fellow enthusiasts, lots of travelling and many happy memories photographing steam locomotives in such exotic locations as Monkwearmouth, Hartlepool and Newcastle (Central). Travelling via Church Fenton and York, our motive power for the Darlington trip was anything but North Eastern, nor even LNER in origin. Typically for the RCTS Nottingham branch something unusual was arranged in the shape of an ex LMS 2P 4-4-0 and a Southern 'Schools' class 4-4-0. Albeit, the locomotive which took the excursion into the confines of the locomotive works had ties to the LNER in the shape of a WD 2-8-0.

Anyway, the trip was a resounding success and all the more so because I managed to borrow a camera from my cousin giving me the opportunity to make a photographic record of the day. By today's standards the camera was by no means a masterpiece of either German or Japanese design but the results it yielded were quite acceptable which in turn spurred me to secure my own instrument with which to record the locomotives and railway scenes in those seemingly, in 1960's, far off places.

Further trips to the southern areas of the NE Region in Yorkshire expanded my photographic portfolio and gave me opportunities to test my skills as a railway photographer. One instance inside Holbeck roundhouse in Leeds saw me setting up a shot in the gloom of the place on an already rainy day, and one particular RCTS member told me in blunt Anglo-Saxon that I had no *#* chance, which to a youngster like myself hit my confidence somewhat. However, on my return home, and with the film developed, I produced a number of prints and set off to the very next RCTS meeting where I gave away copies of the said subject which was, much to the surprise and, I must say, joy of the aforementioned gentleman, perfect.

Since then I have relished the challenge of the internal shots at shed and works alike and I must say that in most cases I have had success. Admitted patience and time itself was required and the short-stop RCTS shed bashes were not the occasions on which to practice my skills. However, my whims were tolerated.

The last year of steam in the North Eastern Region saw me heading northwards in July 1967 to

One of Peter Edgington's scratch built Q7's ready for the return run to Tyne Dock with its soon to be coupled empty iron-ore bogie hopper wagons.

B16 No.61410 at the head of a special passenger working on Peter's NER layout.

opportunity to photograph his layout and herein reproduce a couple of views from it as a tribute to a great friend and fellow enthusiast. He would have been proud to have been associated with this book.

Malcolm Castledine, Long Eaton, 2005.

the engine sheds at West Hartlepool, Sunderland, Tyne Dock, and North and South Blyth. Lineside opportunities were also open to me and although the variety of motive power was not on the scale of previous years by any means with J27's, K1's, Q6's and WD 2-8-0's being the fare on offer, it did not alter the fact that working steam was still available, on this Region of BR at least for a few more weeks. It was during this time in Durham and Northumberland that I noticed, admittedly you couldn't really miss it, the amount of industrial steam still at work, particularly the National Coal Board's Backworth and Burradon system in Northumberland. Seeing those particular railways inspired me to photographically record them too and 1967 turned out to be the start of a long affair with industrial steam.

However, BR steam was still around but would not be for much longer so I concentrated on the big boys knowing that the little chaps would be around the following year and for some years thereafter.

The dereliction of BR locomotives and their surroundings was of no surprise by 1967 but the scale of the mass condemnations still took the breath away. Much of it I have recorded and reproduce here for those who might not have seen it first hand or whom may have forgotten those images from thirty-eight years ago.

My good friend Peter Edgington was a great fan of the North Eastern Railway and during his lifetime built a model railway layout which had a NER flavour, with the majority of the scratch built locomotives being of NER origin. Shortly before he died I had the

Being as it was mainly a depot connected to moving mineral trains, one doesn't usually associate Royston engine shed with Stanier Cl.5's but No.45219 was definately a part of the allocation in November 1965 as were two other ex LMS 4-6-0s, Nos.44912 and 45207. All three had come to Royston (for whatever purpose I don't know) in September 1963 from Low Moor shed. No.44912 left Royston in June 1966 for Holbeck, along with No.45219, but No.45207 stayed on and was withdrawn during September. No.45219 was just thirty years old for this photograph and was one of the 320-odd built by Armstrong Whitworth between 1935 and 1937. Its first shed was Farnley Junction where it arrived in November 1935. From there on it spent most of its working life on the Central Division of the LMS going to Blackpool in June 1936 and in November, for the first time to Southport. In July 1937 it went to Bank Hall but was back in Southport in November. Newton Heath had it for the summer timetable of 1938 and at the end of that period it was returned to Southport. From June 1940 Rose Grove had its services and it did not go back to Southport until September 1942. For the next five years it was resident in the seaside town until October 1947 when it finally departed for the east. Agecroft was its first shed and then in April 1948 Newton Heath got it once again. In October 1950 it crossed the Pennines again and was never to return to Lancashire. Huddersfield was its first post-war shed in Yorkshire but they only kept it for a few weeks and passed it onto Low Moor in November. It worked from Low Moor for the next eleven years and in August 1961 went to Copley Hill of all places, returning to Low Moor in June 1963. Then in September of that year it was off to Royston. It was finally withdrawn in September 1967 at Holbeck shed and ended up at T.W.Ward's scrapyard in Killamarsh in early 1968. Looking healthy enough here, it is keeping company with a Stanier 8F - the more usual fare at Royston - and in the background can be seen Monckton Main Colliery, the reason for this depot's existence.

Compared with most engine sheds on the LMS Midland Division, Royston had a relatively short history being opened as late as 1932. The main function of the depot's allocation was to move the vast tonnage of coal being wound by the local collieries. The shed itself consisted of ten dead-end roads and was built in the style of the period adopted by the LMS to rebuild some of their older establishments whereas each road had its own slated pitched roof. The site was chosen carefully and the installation of a turning triangle surrounding the shed did away with the need for a turntable. The allocation of Royston has always reflection its role and shortly after opening some twenty-nine 0-6-0 tender engines, of various vintages, shared the premises with five Fowler 0-8-0s which were complimented by four 0-6-0Ts. Towards the end of World War Two the allocation had changed somewhat but still had the flavour of freight locomotives; 0-6-0 tender engines were down in number to twenty-four, the 0-8-0s had gone to be replaced by eight Stanier 8F's, four 'Crabs' for mixed traffic work were an addition as were the four ex Midland 4-4-0s, two of which were compounds; three Stanier 2-6-2Ts along with three 2-6-4Ts brought further new duties to the shed. To round off the rather cosmopolitan allocation there was also an ex L&Y 2-4-2T and three former MR 0-4-4Ts. By the time of my visit in November 1965 the allocation had changed somewhat. Gone were the 0-6-0s Midland or otherwise, although the last five had hung around after being condemned the previous month. Stanier 8F's were now the mainstay, assisted by a handful of WD 2-8-0s. There was also four Ivatt moguls, Nos.43076 to 43079, newly arrived from Hull. The one featured here, No.43078, had been at Dairycoates since being built at Darlington in October 1950. Royston was to be its last shed as it was withdrawn in December of the following year; the others went on to other sheds before that time. On the right is long time resident 8F No.48466, one of the Swindon built wartime 8F's which was on loan to Severn Tunnel Junction shed from new in February 1945 to September 1947 when it 'came back' to the LMS at Crewe South shed. It came to Royston from Warrington Dallam in August 1951 and stayed until withdrawal in May 1967. Besides the steam locomotives, the diesels had made inroads onto the Royston allocation albeit only shunters (it seemed that every shed had a couple of them much like a rash, during that period), which comprised a solitary 0-6-0 diesel mechanical and six of the larger 0-6-0 diesel electric type which went on to form BR Class 08 some years later.

Three of the 4F 0-6-0s mentioned earlier, left to right 44056, 43906 and 43968, which had been withdrawn in October but had been stored for many months at Royston shed. There condemnation coincided with the 4F's stored at Normanton and no doubt a directive had gone out to all sheds with these 0-6-0s on the books to condemn them during that month. Note that No.43906 is still showing the legend LMS on its tender which must be something of a record because in 1965 the LMS had ceased to exist some seventeen years previously. How it managed for so long to avoid the painter's brush is anyone's guess but one theory is that tender swapping at sheds was a regular occurrence and most locomotives had two or more different tenders during their lifetime. However, tenders also require maintenance so another mystery is revealed. Less of a mystery is the tender attached to 44056 which is one of the type fitted out with a sliding roof and used when required for snowplough duties. Most of these particular 4F's had a short journey to the scrapman as they mostly went to Station Steel at Wath.

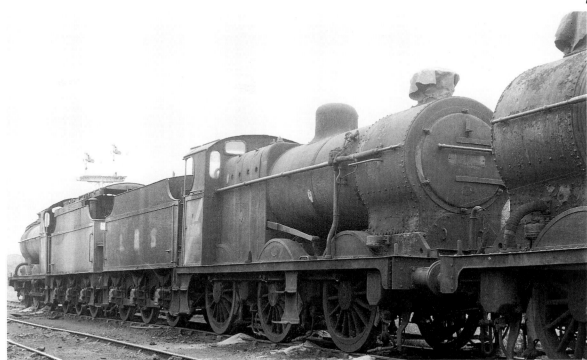

Finding a B1 with nameplates at the end of 1965 was fast becoming 'a needle and haystack' situation but on a visit to Normanton shed on the 7th November I spotted No.61019 NILGHAI of York shed not only in steam but complete with its brasswork, although just to spoil the effect it had no shed plate. Built at Darlington and put into traffic during February 1947, this engine had, except for nine weeks spent at Haymarket shed in late 1948, been a true North Eastern engine. Even its demise in 1967 took place in NE Region territory at draper's in Hull. During its twenty year career it had been allocated to various former North Eastern Railway sheds, some on a number of different occasions: Gateshead (3); Blaydon (2); Heaton (2); Alnmouth (1); Darlington (1); Tweedmouth (1); York (1).

Normanton engine shed had its origins way back in 1850 when the North Midland and the York & North Midland railways erected a shed which was replaced in 1867 by a roundhouse on the site we see here. The polygonal shaped roundhouse was a joint venture by the Midland Railway and the North Eastern. Later, in 1882 the MR built a five road straight shed for their own use and for the locomotives of the Lancashire & Yorkshire Railway. This 'joint' facility continued throughout the period of Grouping and into BR days although by then the former NER contingent had dropped somewhat in numbers and LMS types tended to predominate. The old polygon shed was demolished in the mid 1930's to make way for mechanical coal and ash plants installed by the LMS. In this November 1965 view of the area around the coaling plant we are virtually stood on the site of the erstwhile polygon shed although by then all trace had long been obliterated except for a slight curvature in the embankment on the east side of the site. Resident Cl.4 2-6-4T No.42083 appears to be on shed duties, a rather mundane occupation for a capable mixed traffic tank engine but at least it is employed and would be for another eighteen months or so. This is one of the Brighton built ex LMS designs which BR were still producing, even though the BR Standard designs had started to appear, into the early 1950's. No.42083 actually went into traffic at the same time as the first of the Standard engines, No.70000 BRITANNIA. Many of the Brighton built engines started their working life at Southern Region sheds and this one was no exception being put to work at Stewarts Lane shed in January 1951. Fourteen months later it made the break from the Southern and went to the North Eastern Region at Selby shed. During the following May it went to Scarborough by Darlington shed needed it from July. After three years and two months there it went back to the seaside but this time to Whitby and at the end of the season, in September 1955. Nearly four years later in July 1959 it was reallocated to Sowerby Bridge which was quite a change but somebody had to go there. Normanton, its last shed and home for the rest of its life, beckoned in February 1962.

This melancholy line-up of ex LMS 4F 0-6-0s at Normanton in November 1965 is headed by 44400 with 44408, 44458 and 44170 tucked in behind. All of them had been withdrawn during the previous month and were destined to travel together to the same Chesterfield scrap merchant, Garnham Harris & Elton, who purchased them all in December. These were the last of the ex LMS 0-6-0 tender engines at allocated to Normanton and their passing severed a long relationship between Derby designs and the engine shed. As an aside, only one of the four was actually built at Derby - No.44408 in 1927. No.44170 was a 1926 Crewe built engine whilst No.44400 was built by the North British Loco. Co. in 1927. No.44458, the youngest of the bunch was built at Horwich in 1928. Quite a diverse beginning for such a small group which were reputedly all the same, however, in a class some five hundred and seventy-five strong there was bound to be instances such as this all over the place. Perhaps if three of the others which had been built by either St Rollox, Andrew Barclay, and Kerr, Stuart had been in the line-up we might have attained something of a unique record. Behind the 4F's is the brick built boiler house associated with the abortive 1947 Fuel Oil programme. Beyond that is the coaling plant with its companion ash plant and in the right distance is the five road engine shed. The mineral wagons in the yards behind reminds us that we were in mining country.

The former Lancashire & Yorkshire Railway engine shed at Wakefield, latterly known as 56A, was usually, during BR days, associated with the WD Austerity 2-8-0's of which the shed had one of the largest allocations in the country. However, in November 1965 when I visited the place, two ex LMS 'Jubilees', Nos.45694 BELLEROPHON, and 45739 ULSTER, were allocated. Previously two other Stanier 6P's had been and gone, No.45589 GWALIOR, which arrived in June 1964 was condemned in March 1965. the other was No.45602 BRITISH HONDURAS, which had the shortest stay, arriving in September 1964 and departing for Holbeck during the following month. This view of 45694 on 7th November has 45739 in the right background and towering over the pair of them is the 500 ton coaling plant which had been a feature of this shed since 1932 when the shed yard was extended southwards. No.45694 was one of the Crewe works batch built in 1936 and put into traffic at Crewe North shed in March of that year. By July it was resident at Preston shed but just over a year later it moved to the Midland Division at Kentish Town shed. During the early part of WW2 it moved to Derby and later, in July 1942 to Holbeck. During the last month of the Big Four it moved to Barrow Road shed in Bristol but two months later in February 1948 it went back to Holbeck from where it worked until June 1962 when reallocation took it to Low Moor. Wakefield acquired it in February 1965 and after nearly two years it was withdrawn for scrap in February 1967. No.45739 which had arrived at Wakefield in June 1964 was withdrawn at the same time.

(left) On 7th November 1965 Class 4MT 2-6-4T No.42150 was laid up at Wakefield shed with its leading coupled wheels absent, a rather precarious existence in late 1965. However, the wheels were eventually reinstalled and the seventeen year old engine continued in service until its December 1966 withdrawal. From new in May 1948, this Derby built tank had been working from another former L&Y shed at Sowerby Bridge and came to Wakefield in June 1962.

(opposite) The one thing that struck you on a visit to Wakefield shed, and I suppose any BR engine shed during the 'run-down' years, was the external condition of the locomotives. This forlorn 'Crab' is Stockport Edgeley's No.42942 which was a regular visitor to these parts probably having returned coal empties. Likewise many of Wakefield's own allocation took trains (usually coal) over the Pennines on a daily basis. The 2-6-0, in the company of an unidentified B1, had been at 9B since December 1960 and some four months after this view was captured it moved to Birkenhead. Withdrawal in January 1967, No.42942 was amongst the last of the Hughes/Fowler 'Crabs'.

(right) Another Derby built Class 4MT 2-6-4T at Wakefield in November 1965 was No.42161 sandwiched between a B1 and an Ivatt 2-6-0. This particular engine had seen a more varied life since being put into traffic at Wigan Central shed in August 1948 and just a few weeks later it was sent south to St Albans shed from where it worked until February 1954 when it moved to Nottingham shed. Trafford Park shed acquired it on loan from December 1958 until the following January when it returned to Nottingham. During September 1963 it was reallocated to Rowsley then, in May 1964 to Leicester Midland shed. Later that year, in the November, it went to Derby but in February 1965 Wakefield got it. Another November move, later in the year, saw 42161 allocated to Darlington of all places but it was, after all, part of the North Eastern Region. Finally, in January 1966 it came back to Yorkshire but this time to Holbeck where, in December that year it was condemned. It was purchased for scrap by T.W.Ward at Killamarsh in March 1967.

On the closure of Ardsley shed in October 1965, many of its engines were condemned and amongst those was Gresley V2 No.60923. Over the next few weeks that shed site was cleared of all its 'dead' locomotives with many being sold to scrap merchants. No.60923 was acquired by J.Cashmore at Great Bridge, and en route to their West Midlands yard, the V2 stopped over at Wakefield shed for a few days. Luckily I saw and photographed it, noting that except for the missing front numberplate, it was virtually intact. As late as February of the previous year this engine had undergone a General overhaul at Darlington works but no matter what mechanical condition it was in it was in the wrong place at the wrong time although inevitably time would have caught up with it no matter which shed it called home. Built at Darlington in wartime, 60923 or No.4894 to give it its proper number of the period, went to Heaton shed in November 1941 and then Gateshead in March 1943. Nearly twenty years later, on 2nd December 1962, it moved to Ardsley and its eventual demise.

B1's at Wakefield became a common sight during the last dozen years before the shed closed. Besides all the visiting examples there were many actually allocated to the establishment. Nos.61017 (now without its BUSHBUCK nameplates) was a visitor from York but No.61131 was a resident on the 7th November 1965. Both engines had 'done the rounds' of the sheds during their somewhat brief careers. No.61131 had come to Wakefield from Ardsley at the end of March 1963 after a four month stay at the ex Great Northern shed prior to which it had spent its first spell at Wakefield. New from NBL Co. in February 1947 it had been at Gorton and then to Woodford in June of that year. Two years later it was sent to Colwick and in September 1952 it went for a five week period to Stratford after which it came to the West Riding and its first allocation to Ardsley shed. After five years there it moved across to Bradford Hammerton Street but was forced to reallocate to nearby Low Moor in January 1958 when the ex GNR shed closed to steam. Just over one year later it went to Wakefield. Darlington built No.61017 had also come into traffic in early 1947 going first to York shed and then in early 1948 to Neville Hill. In February 1949 it moved to Stockton and four and a half years later back to Leeds Neville Hill. York was next, again, and from November 1955 to June 1958 it worked out of 50A. On 8th June 1958 Copley Hill got its services for an eight month period before it went to Wakefield. From 25th November 1962 Ardsley had it until its final move to York in October 1965. Condemned in November 1966, it was sold to Draper's in Hull during January 1967. No.61131, which was condemned a month later, also ended up at Draper's being sold to the yard in February. Note the roof of the engine shed which was revamped by BR in 1955.

(*opposite*) The former Midland Railway engine shed at Leeds Holbeck became part of the North Eastern Region in January 1957 and from that day was coded 55A. Essentially Holbeck did not have any significant changes of motive power or mass evictions and kept its large stud of 'Jubilees', the handful of 'Royal Scots' and most of the other ex LMS types previously associated with the depot. Only in the 1960's did anything 'unusual' arrive and that was in the shape of a few Gresley A3's drafted in to help out on the Settle & Carlisle workings. On 7th November 1965 steam power was still very much in evidence and 4-6-0 tender engines still graced the twin roundhouses just as they had done since the 'Claughton's' arrived in the late 1920's. The lofty roof of the original square roundhouses, dating from 1868, gave off a somewhat 'church like' ambience, with smoke. LMS Cl.5 No.44857, just caught on the edge of the picture, had been a resident of 55A since its September 1945 move from Bristol Barrow Road. New from Crewe in December 1944, its initial shed had been Wellingborough but in August 1945 it transferred to Bristol. Three months before being withdrawn in September 1967, No.44857 moved to its last shed at Normanton and from there it was all down hill. Jubilee No.45574, which had no nameplates at the time of my visit, had previously been named INDIA but had recently lost those plates, probably before its arrival at Holbeck in the previous May. One of the North British Loco. Co. built 'Jubilees', 45574 started its working life at Upperby shed in September 1934 and just a month later was transferred to Aston for six months before moving to Shrewsbury for a few weeks stay. Then it was down to Camden where it managed a two year stint. In May 1937 it went to Blackpool Central shed and worked from there until the run down of the shed prior to closure in late 1964. Back to Carlisle but this time to Kingmoor shed, it stayed until the following May when 55A beckoned. Standard Cl.4 No.75057 was a visitor from Skipton shed and from new in March 1957 it had been at Leicester Midland shed then, in September 1962, it moved to Derby. Fourteen months later it was reallocated to Springs Branch depot at Wigan and finally in May 1965 to Skipton. Withdrawal took place in February 1966 just a few months before Skipton engine shed closed and just a month short of the engine's ninth birthday.

The illusion of stained glass windows strengthens the cathedral like qualities inside Holbeck shed but, on taking a closer look, it will seen that the stained glass is smoke stained and where it appears to be clean and clear it is in fact missing. On 7th November 1965, after nearly one hundred years service, the shed was slowly giving up and falling apart. Closure of the roundhouses came in October 1967 when steam was also banished. Demolition of the roundhouses followed shortly afterwards but a diesel depot was created utilising the old repair shop on the south side of the shed yard. Derby built Class 4 tank No.42052 had no need to worry about eviction when the end came for 55A as it would have been withdrawn long before then in May 1967. since being built in 1950 this engine been at Bradford Manningham shed until January 1959 when it came to Holbeck. In December 1966 it returned to Manningham until closure of that shed in April 1967 when it came back to Holbeck for the last time.

Another resident tank engine at Holbeck during my November 1965 visit was this Derby built Fowler 2-6-4 Cl.4 tank which came into traffic just a year before 'Jubilee' No.45574. After a career which saw it spend much of its life in South Wales working around the Swansea area, it went to Birkenhead in August 1962 but eventually got away from it's Great Western associations when it arrived at Holbeck in December 1963. Withdrawn in June 1966, this was the penultimate engine of its type in service. Draper's of Hull purchased it for scrap shortly after withdrawal.

(opposite) Leeds Neville Hill shed, 7th November 1965 with ex North Eastern Q6 No.63426 resting in familiar surroundings. The former North Eastern shed at Neville Hill was opened in 1894 and consisted of four roundhouses, in line on a roughly north-south axis. British Railways modernised the depot during the 1950's demolishing two of the sheds and reroofing the others, at the same time making provision for diesel locomotive servicing. Besides the four turntables in the roundhouses, there was also a 55ft appliance, and water column, in the yard for engines arriving at the Down sidings which did not require to go on shed before their return journey. Neville Hill depot closed to steam on 12th June 1966 and is still in the business of servicing today's motive power. Note the exLMS 2-6-4T on the right which ten years previously would have been a rare visitor indeed to this depot but by this time any demarcation lines that had existed in Leeds, regarding regional boundaries and old company locomotive types, had been abolished and virtually anything could be seen anywhere. During the late 1950's and early 60's no less than twelve former LMS 2-6-4 tank engines had been allocated to Neville Hill. The Armstrong Whitworth built Q6 had started life at Blaydon shed in April 1920 and, apart from a couple of weeks spent at Borough Gardens in November 1931, it had worked from the Tyneside shed until moving south to Darlington in June 1941. Another wartime move in March 1943 saw the engine allocated to Stockton and four years later it crossed the Tees into North Yorkshire for an eleven year stint at Newport. When that shed was closed in June 1958, to make way for the construction of Tees yard, 63426 went to the newly opened Thornaby shed at the western end of that marshalling yard. In December 1962 it arrived at Neville Hill for a three and a half year stay before moving to Normanton. By now steam motive power was being chased into all sorts of corners and after less than four months at Normanton it departed northwards in October 1966 to its last shed - Tyne Dock. Back on Tyneside, its work was somewhat sporadic and going the way of everything steam on the North Eastern Region in 1967 it was withdrawn on 22nd June. Ironically, and considering that scrapyards were fairly prevalent in the area, this engine was sold to a yard in Chesterfield, Derbyshire in the August and that's where another former NER 0-8-0 ended its illustrious forty-seven year life.

The former Lancashire & Yorkshire Railway engine shed at Low Moor, south of Bradford, became part of the North Eastern Region and was given the code 56F from September 1956. Although all the former LMS sheds in Yorkshire eventually became part of either the NE Region or the Eastern Region, the change was not implemented at the same time. Those former Midland sheds for instance under the old LMS shed code 20 did not become part of the Region until February 1957, nor did the former LNWR shed at Hillhouse, Huddersfield. However, once the boundaries and resulting paperwork was sorted out the change was hardly discernible at first and then familiar locomotives began to move away overnight and different ones took their place but, the regional changes had come at a time of motive power transition anyway on British Railways. At Low Moor shed the former LMS types continued to be in the majority but certain former LNER classes began to muscle in or as was more likely, came there looking for a home. The shed was one of the last ones in Yorkshire to close to steam and that event took place on the last day of September 1967, just before steam in general was officially banished from the Region. Opened in 1888, Low Moor consisted a dead-ended twelve road shed with a northlight roof. However, by the time British Railways came into being the allocation had been cut by at least third from the L&Y days and consequently when the shed needed a new roof only the eastern six roads were recovered. The other half of the shed was left open to the elements and four of the roads were abandoned. This view, on the very wet and dark afternoon of 7th November 1965, shows a line of 'out of service' B1's stored on the extreme western road of the old shed, the wall of which was still blocking the view from the railway houses on the other side. The identified B1's, from left to right were: 61016, now nameless but formerly carrying the name INYALA. This engine had come to Low Moor from Mirfield in April 1964 and had been withdrawn just seven days prior to my visit. It was purchased for scrap in December by Hughes, Bolckow at Blyth, at the other end of the region. The next one in line, No.61110 was not a Low Moor engine, its last shed before withdrawal on 31st October, being Ardsley. It too was destined for the same scrapyard in the north-east. Ardsley's No.61353 was next and this B1 had been condemned on 16th August and had already been sold to the same scrapyard as the other two Thompson engines. No doubt they would form a cavalcade when the time came to move up north.

On 22nd October 1966 the British Transport Police personnel at York station had their hands full containing the enthusiasm of literally a couple of thousand 'trainspotters' as we were called. Probably, if truth be known, we were given many other less gracious titles that day. However, railwaymania 1960's style had arrived and the platform end scenes captured here were to be repeated virtually every weekend at different locations throughout the country until August 1968. The reason for this gathering was to record the arrival, on a special from the north, of 'Merchant Navy' No.35026 LAMPORT & HOLT LINE. Now up to that particular date in 1966 Southern Region Pacifics had been fairly rare visitors to York. In fact it would be safe to say that since the Locomotive Exchanges of 1948 the number of Bullied engines seen this far north was basically nil; hence the excitement shown and the amount of film exposed. Here the A.R.E.S. *THE ELIZABETHAN* special has just come to a halt and No.35026 will detach to be replaced by preserved A3 No.4472 FLYING SCOTSMAN. There are two locomotive types which are dear to my heart - the Gresley A3's and the Bullied Pacifics - so as you can surmise I was on Cloud Nine that day.

The view looking south towards Holgate bridge as the 'Merchant Navy' is released from the train and makes its way to shed. In the background No.4472 awaits the signal to reverse onto the special and take it on to London. The autumn weather was far from glorious but spirits were in no way dampened. Never mind sergeant only twenty-two months of this before you get your railway back.

(opposite, top) Earlier in the day FLYING SCOTSMAN was prepared on York shed and in this view adjacent to the wet ash pits, the Pacific is waiting to move onto the station. At this period, the A3 had the second tender attached which gave the engine greater endurance between stops on the main line. This tender was converted to carry only water and it was also equipped with a corridor to give the crew access to any train being hauled by 4472. I rather like this particular view of the engine as it seems to me to convey the majesty and elegance to these superb engines.

(opposite, bottom) A rear three-quarter view of No.4472 and tender's at York shed, showing the corridor connection on the second (water) tender. In the background the blurred image of what would eventually become another in the long line of the ECML 'greats' - the Deltics - passes on a northbound working.

In an effort to inject a little bit of modern image - 1960's style - into this album I have included this scene of the south end of the Up main lines at York station on 5th August 1963. I must admit that diesels did not figure prominently on any but a tiny handful of the thousands of exposures I made over the years and English Electric Vulcan Foundry built Type 4 D275 only got onto this particular one because of the Peppercorn K1, No.62065, which was just passing through the station. The first thing to note is that the diesel locomotive is as filthy as the steam locomotive, a reflection of the period when Cleaners, the bottom of the ladder in the locomotive footplate hierarchy, were difficult to recruit. The 1960's did offer a much wider range of employment other than the railways and certainly much of that was not only cleaner and less dangerous but also better paid. What of the motive power ? Well the Vulcan Foundry built diesel was already over three years old and was based at the time, I think, at York depot so it is possible that the train it is heading originated at York and could have been bound for anywhere south and west of Yorkshire. Eventually D275 became 40075 and ended up at Gateshead depot from where, in December 1981, it was withdrawn. However, it languished at various sites until February 1987 when it was finally cut up at the erstwhile Vic Berry yard in Leicester. The K1 was only ten years older than the diesel and it still had nearly four years of life left in it and all of it from York shed where it was condemned in March 1967. It ended up at Draper's yard in Hull being cut up on 28th August 1967. Prior to its reallocation to York in August 1959, the K1 had started its working life at Darlington shed, ex NBL Co. 23rd January 1950, from there, at the end of June 1950 it moved east to Stockton where it spent the greater part of its life. In June 1959 it went to Low Moor of all places but within ten weeks it was back amongst friends at York.

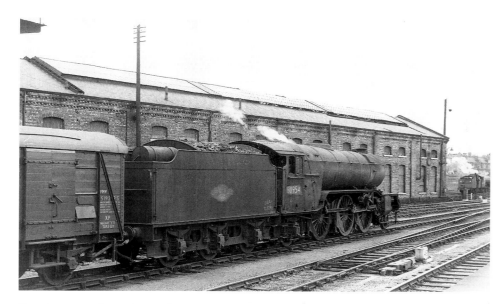

V2 No.60954 shunting York station on 6th August 1963. Note the Southern Region PMV (S1929S) next to the engine. Was this van bound for a south coast resort such as Bournemouth? This was the last summer when the V2's were still working in great numbers, note the V2 in the background on main line stand-by duties, and No.60954 was enjoying its last fling before entering Darlington works for scrapping in December. From new in September 1942, this Darlington built engine had been allocated throughout its twenty-one year life to York North shed. It was condemned on 18th November and its last repair had been a Casual Heavy carried out at Darlington where, from 1951, all its overhauls were done. Prior to that, Doncaster works had been responsible.

Coming northwards under Holgate bridge and into York on the same day was V2 No.60864 at the head of an all LMS stock Liverpool-Newcastle express. The V2 would have taken over this train at Leeds (City), taking it on to Newcastle, the ten bogie load hardly taxing this capable engine. This was another York V2 although it did not have the same unbroken period of time allocated to the shed. Released to traffic from Darlington at the end of June 1939, it went first to York then, in November 1944, it moved to Darlington shed for four years, returning to York in December 1948. In June 1959 Copley Hill shed had its services until the following November when it returned to York. Withdrawn on 16th March 1964, it too went to Darlington for cutting up, entering works on 9th April.

Looking across the turntable inside one of the York roundhouses on 21st May 1966 with, what was then, a typical line-up of steam locomotives which could be found at the depot. Left to right are Thompson B1 No.61035 which had carried the name PRONGHORN but was by now bereft of the nameplates. The B1 was a York engine having come to the depot in the previous October from Gateshead shed. This was the engines' second stint at York, its first when new from Darlington works in October 1947. Six months after that it moved to Neville Hill shed in Leeds where it stayed until January 1961 when it went to Blaydon. Two years later it transferred to Heaton before moving on to Gateshead four month after that. No.61035 was condemned at the end of 1966 and was sold for scrap to Albert Draper in Hull the following February. Next in the line was a Darlington built Ivatt LMS 4F mogul, No.43097 which went to Selby when new in January 1951. In October 1959 it went to the former Lancashire & Yorkshire shed at Goole, arriving at York in July 1962. The engine had one more move before withdrawal and that was to North Blyth shed in August 1966 where in the latter months of steam motive power in the north-east it joined other class members moving the coal from the collieries to the staiths before the diesels took over for good. However, No.43097 was withdrawn in January 1967, long before steam was abolished on the North Eastern Region. Peppercorn K1 No.62028 was slightly older than the

Ivatt mogul but only by about eighteen months. This North British Loco. Co. built engine was, like many of the class, first allocated to Blaydon shed when new in 1949. from there it went to Gateshead in May 1962 before moving the York, its last shed, in September 1963. Withdrawn six months after this scene was captured on film, 62028 was sold for scrap to Arnott Young at Parkgate & Rawmarsh. Finally we have another Darlington built Ivatt mogul, No.43071. It had a more varied allocation history than 43097 and worked from sheds the length and breadth of what became the NE Region. Starting at Darlington in September 1950, it went to Wakefield in May 1955. A year later it went to North Blyth for four months before going even further north to Alnmouth. By the end of June 1957 it was at Middlesbrough, moving into the new shed at Thornaby the following summer. In November 1958 Selby had it on the books until it moved over to Dairycoates in October of the next year. Later that month it transferred to York and finally in August 1966, along with 43097 it went back to North Blyth and was withdrawn in March 1967, just seventeen years old. Arnott Young at Dinsdale purchased the engine for scrap in December 1967. No.43097 went to Hull eventually but only as a 59 ton piece of scrap acquired by Drapers.

Still operational on Saturday 21st May 1966, V2 No.60831 is in the hands of the boilersmiths in York roundhouse who appear to be sorting out a problem with the superheater. One of the pre-war V2's, 60831 worked the ECML during the conflict but after nationalisation it went in May 1949 to work on the former Great Central main line and was based in the first place at Woodford. In March 1953 it went to Leicester Central shed but in May it went 'on loan' to King's Cross shed until the end of June because six other V2's had been loaned to the Southern Region during a motive power 'emergency' when their 'Merchant Navy' and 'West Country' Pacifics were temporarily withdrawn. On return to GC lines, the V2 went back to Woodford and it was not until 1st September 1957 that it finally got back to Leicester Central shed. After two years there, it came to York and was condemned on 6th December 1966. Too late to be cut up at either Darlington or Doncaster, the engine was sold to Drapers in Hull during February 1967. Note that 60831 has separate cylinders, one of only seventy-one of the class to be changed from the original monobloc casting.

It was always nice to see V2's and York was the place to go to photograph them. Showing its right flank is No.60886, one of the class which had separate cylinders, and which had been at York shed since early December 1962. From being built at Darlington and coming into traffic in November 1939, this engine had, up to its move to York, worked only from sheds in the north-east of England with Heaton having the lion's share of its time on four different occasions, followed by Gateshead which had it twice and, for a seven month period in 1951, Tweedmouth also had its services. In this 21st May 1966 view, the engine appears to be in reasonable condition externally but it was in fact withdrawn, having been condemned during the previous month. In June it was sold for scrap to the J.Cashmore yard at Great Bridge.

On the same day No.60806 was still operational and was receiving a boiler wash-out. Reallocated to York in January 1966 from Darlington shed, this was another V2 which had spent much of its life working from sheds in the north-east although from new August 1937 it was at York until March 1943 when it went to Gateshead to start its twenty-three year association with the former North Eastern sheds. Besides those sheds mentioned in 60886's caption, No.60806 also served for a year West Hartlepool of all places from June 1963 to July 1964. Prior to that it had spent three years at the new Thornaby depot. Condemned on 4th September, this engine also ended up at the same Great Bridge scrapyard. The tender on the left belonged to former LMS Cl.5 No.45339 of Newton Heath shed. The visiting 4-6-0 was actually the same age as the V2 but it continued working until June 1967.

In LNER days this roundhouse at York (North) shed would have been No.4 shed with No.3 shed and its electrically powered 60ft turntable just beyond and in the background here. My vantage point is the 70ft turntable and on 15th April 1967 two resident steam locomotives, both B1's, stand side by side in their stalls. To the left is twenty years old No.61021, by now nameless but formerly REITBOK, which came to York in September 1960 from Wakefield. Its days were numbered and on 6th June it was condemned. Alongside is No.61337 which had come to York in October 1948. Though only two months old at the time, York was the B1's third shed and it wasn't to be its last because as late as 25th June 1967 it was allocated to Low Moor shed where, three months later, it was withdrawn. In No.3 shed a number of York's decent sized stud of diesel mechanical shunters congregate around the turntable.

The diesel depot at York, fashioned from two of the old roundhouses when the depot underwent massive reconstruction in the 1950's, was adjacent to the main line and it was in here, in April 1967, that preserved A4 No.60019 BITTERN was stabled for safekeeping. Surrounded as it was by more modern forms of motive power, the 'Streak' still looked magnificent.

A visit to York shed on 15th April 1967 found ex LMS 'Jubilee' No.45562 ALBERTA resting in one of the roundhouse stalls. This Holbeck based engine was by now relegated to secondary services and was being used on a regular basis for passing out firemen on the daily Newcastle to Manchester (Red Bank) empty newspaper van train. The fact that firemen were still being passed out, when the abolition of steam on British Railways was just over a year away seems somewhat ironic especially when so many footplatemen were being made redundant all over the system on a somewhat weekly basis. From new in August 1934, No.45562 had been at Preston shed for nearly two years until moving to Longsight in June 1936 for a four month spell before a move to Rugby. That reallocation lasted only four months also and ALBERTA went back to the Manchester area but this time to Patricroft shed. After six months it moved yet again, now to Holbeck but on a more permanent basis, staying until March 1964. A short spell at Farnley Junction saw it return to Holbeck in time for withdrawal in November 1967.

Stoke based Stanier 8F No.48291 heads a line of freight locomotives at York on 21st May 1966. Originally built for the Ministry of Supply as WD No.404, then later as 70404, this 2-8-0 was taken into British Railways stock in December 1949. Its first shed was Crewe South where it had a ten year stay. In August 1959 it moved to Nuneaton then in March 1964 back to Crewe South shed, and from there to Stoke in December. This May 1966 foray to York must have been amongst its last so far north as the following month it was withdrawn and by October was the property of Ward's scrapyard at Beighton.

On the shed yard at York (North) on 21st May 1966 were a number of redundant A1's, No.60124 can be seen on the extreme right, and in amongst them, alongside the ash pits, was a less elegant and extremely filthy Ivatt Cl.4 No.43123 which had recently been reallocated from West Hartlepool. During October this engine was sent to North Blyth shed from where it was withdrawn in July 1967.

Thompson A2/3 No.60512 STEADY AIM had been a York engine since December 1952 but within six months of this picture being taken at York North shed, it had undergone a Casual Light repair at Doncaster and moved to the Scottish Region along with 60522 STRAIGHT DEAL and 60524 HERRINGBONE. All three were initially based at St Margarets shed and their move north probably gave them an extension of a few more years of operational life. In September 1963 all three A2/3's went to Polmadie shed of all places. On 14th June 1965 it was reallocated to Dundee Tay Bridge shed but probably never arrived there as five days after its move 'on paper' it was condemned along with the 60522 and the pair were then sold to Motherwell Machinery & Scrap Co. in July. They were the last of the class. No.60524 had been condemned in the previous February and sold to the same scrap merchants in May. For some reason Thompson never did get his Pacific types quite right, the position of the outside cylinders especially did not do anything for their looks.

From 1943 to 1946 all the B16's were allocated to York as part of the wartime measures by the LNER to cut down on the number of locomotive types allocated to any particular depot in a bid to reduce the distribution of spares - a quick fix method of 'standardisation' at least to depot level. Once the conflict was over the B16's began to disperse to other sheds in the North Eastern Area but York maintained a sizeable stud of the 4-6-0s until their demise in the early 1960's. No.61475 had been at York since March 1943 having been at Heaton shed from new in March 1920 until October 1934 when it moved to Dairycoates. On 13th January 1963 it moved back to Dairycoates but only briefly as on 15th April it was condemned and went to Darlington works for scrapping on 22nd May. This view of the engine at York in May 1962 shows it in its final form as a B16 Part 2. Its first BR number 61406 was required for the growing class of Thompson B1's and so on 13th December 1949 it was renumbered to 61475.

Q6 No.63459 at York on Saturday 15th April 1967. This, the last of the Armstrong Whitworth built Q6's, was actually the last member to join the class being built in March 1921 and put to traffic at Borough Gardens shed shortly afterwards. Here the engine is en route to Albert Draper's scrapyard in Hull having journeyed down from Tyne Dock, its last shed, where it had been withdrawn in the previous October. It looks as though the souvenir hunters and metal 'collectors' have already taken anything which was easily removable.

Its winter sojourn at Tyne Dock shed has enhanced the dilapidation and corrosion which has a grip of 63459, the tender especially looking the worse for wear. However, one month from being captured on film here, the cutter's torch would go about its work reducing the engine and tender to small pieces of scrap metal. This Q6 spent most of its life working in the north-east although on Christmas Eve 1925 it was reallocated to Doncaster where it stayed until the following August when it returned to Borough Gardens until moved to Tyne Dock in March 1940. Three years later it went to Newport then, in March 1948 it was reallocated to Stockton. Staying on Teesside, in June 1950 a move to Middlesbrough was authorised. August 1954 saw the engine allocated to West Auckland for a nine year stint. In October 1963 it moved into Northumberland, residing at North Blyth shed until December 1965 when it made its final move. Its last 'General' overhaul and indeed its last repair, had taken place during the latter half of 1962 and one can be fairly certain that no cleaning rags had touched its bodywork since it had left Darlington works on that fifth day of October 1962.

Other engines resting around the 70ft turntable of the old No.4 shed on 15th April 1967 were B1 No.61189, BR Standard Cl.3 No.77012 and Peppercorn K1 No.62001. The B1 had, for most of its life, carried the name SIR WILLIAM GRAY and was a recent acquisition for York shed from Wakefield. Less than a month from the date of this photograph it was condemned and sold in July to Draper's scrapyard in Hull. The Standard would also succumb in June, being sold to a Chesterfield yard. No.62001 another newcomer to York, came from West Hartlepool. Condemned on 25th April, it too was also bound for Draper's, being cut up on 28th August 1967.

K1 No.62012 was another 'dead' engine seen on my 15th April 1967 visit to York. It was reallocated to Sunderland at the end of the month and on 17th May it was condemned only to return south for cutting up at drapers scrapyard in Hull on 28th August. Prior to its inglorious end, this K1 had something of a wanderlust starting when it left the NBL Co. in Glasgow and arriving at Gorton shed on 1st July 1949. After nearly a year there it went further south to March in Cambridgeshire and regularly worked freight from that place into London via the former Great Eastern lines. In February 1952 the 'call of the wild' came and 62012 worked northwards until it got to the West Highland line and took up a ten year, six month residence at Fort William shed. Displaced from Scotland by dieselisation, it went to Alnmouth in December 1962 and then onto York in September 1964. Note the ten year old Drewery 0-6-0DM shunter on the right which spent most of its short life at Hammerton Street shed in Bradford. By September 1970 it too would be a pile of scrap but in a different Yorkshire yard.

Pictured at York shed whilst en route to Draper's scrapyard in Hull on 21st May 1966 was Peppercorn A1 No.60124, formerly KENILWORTH. Withdrawn 27th March 1966 at Darlington shed, this was the last Peppercorn A1 in service. Besides the lack of name and number plates, this engine has also lost its chimney.

Just to the south of York station on the west side of the main line, virtually opposite the former railway museum site, was a group of three old engine sheds known as York South. Two of the building were pure roundhouses of North Eastern origin whilst the three road straight shed had at one time been a Great Northern shed. By the early 1960's the sheds had largely fallen into disuse as running sheds although the ex GN shed was regularly stabling ex LMS engines as it had done since the late 1920's. The roundhouses had become dumps for stored and withdrawn engines whilst the straight shed had become something of an annexe of York North shed with the overflow of steam locomotives stabled there. This view of the place on Monday 5th August 1963 shows a WD, V2 No.60963 and a BR Standard Cl.2, sharing the yard with others. V2 No.60963 was condemned on 29th June 1965 and was sold during the following August to Cashmore's at Great Bridge. Built at Darlington and entering traffic on 12th January 1943, this engine was the first Darlington built locomotive to display a works plate with a number, Darlington No.1903 in this case. After stints at Heaton, Gateshead and Darlington, the engine ended up at York, arriving on Boxing Day 1948. Keeping its original cylinder block to withdrawal, the engine acquired a double chimney in February 1960, ATC during 1958 and 1959 and finally a speedometer at its last General repair in October 1962. The BR Standard was probably only passing through or it may have worked into York but none of them were ever allocated to 50A so perhaps this engine was only finding stabling room.

The Permanent Way Engineers yard at York was a large place covering quite a few acres and locomotives could always be found inside its boundaries either collecting, bringing or sorting trains of rails, sleepers, concrete trackside paraphernalia and basically anything BR required to keep the railway working safely and comfortably. On 21st May 1966 two engines waiting to remove a train out of the yard for some weekend lineside work could not have been so dissimilar. Ivatt Class 4MT No.43055 was a 1950 vintage Doncaster product whilst between it and the train was J27 No.65823, which was some forty-two years older and a product of the North British Locomotive Co. Their ages in 1966 would put them on a par with a footplate crew of the period perhaps - the sixteen year old 'passed cleaner' learning the ropes from a fifty-eight year old driver who was probably working the "Old man's link" or some similarly titled group. The mogul had only been at York for a month and would not be staying much longer because in July it moved to South Blyth shed and three months later to North Blyth where it worked out its last year. When new in September 1950 it went to Darlington shed and in January 1952 to West Hartlepool. Kirkby Stephen got it in May 1955 and then Gateshead shed some thirteen months later. At five months it moved across the Tyne to Heaton shed where it completed its one year stay in Newcastle. Holbeck shed, which had recently become part of the North Eastern Region, got it in June 1957 and then it first stay at York started in October 1959 and lasted just over six years. A move back to West Hartlepool in November 1965 was short lived and during that month it returned to Darlington until March 1966 when shed closure forced it back to West Hartlepool for a month before it went back to York. Withdrawal came in July 1967 with a local scrap merchant undoing what Doncaster works had done seventeen years before.

J27 No.65823 although more than three times older than the Ivatt 2-6-0 had very few moves in its lifetime. Its first shed was Sunderland and after some forty-eight years there it went to Borough Gardens in September 1956. Three years later it was back at Sunderland. Its move to York took place in February 1965 and five months after this picture was taken it went north again but this time to South Blyth. However, it seems that its spiritual home must have been Sunderland because on 5th March 1967 it returned for the last time and was condemned two weeks later. It was sold 4th July to Hughes, Bolckow at Blyth, one year short of its 60th birthday.

The driver and fireman of J27 No.65823 were a pleasant and pair, their ages and disposition being nothing like the descriptive hypothesis in the caption concerning No.43055. Although not the most comfortable workplace, the cab of the 0-6-0 was kept immaculate, as was their uniforms. The driver wore a collar and tie, showing off his badge of office, and his boots, as can be seen, were a credit. The mid 1960s and the coming of the end for steam were most likely the last years when enginemen had that air of pride about themselves and their occupation being encouraged one way or another by middle management who had a similar outlook on life and work.

On Sunday 13th May 1962, I was lucky enough to take part in the RCTS East Midlands branch special from Nottingham to Darlington. These trains were aptly named *THE EAST MIDLANDER* and their organisation, itinerary and chosen motive power were all subject to careful planning and some imagination by certain members of the branch. On this occasion the motive power from Nottingham to Darlington was a 1928 Derby built ex LMS 2P 4-4-0 No.40646 and Southern Region 'Schools' class 4-4-0 No.30925 CHELTENHAM; both engines being turned out in superb external condition. At Darlington the special was taken into the BR locomotive works by WD Austerity No.90348 which had recently undergone a heavy repair and was therefore repainted and looking rather splendid for a WD. In this late afternoon view the special is ready to depart south for home with its 'different' motive power.

WD No.90348, the other motive power participant in *THE EAST MIDLANDER* special of May 1962. This engine was from Wakefield shed at the time and was virtually ready to return home, no doubt the working of the special was part of the running-in process necessary after major repairs. In October 1966 No.90348 moved to Sunderland South Dock shed and was withdrawn in September of the following year.

Seen on Darlington Bank Top shed that day was Peppercorn K1 No.62064 which had just completed a 'General' on the 9th May after entering works on 2nd April. Darlington shed was home for the K1 anyway so its running-in would be closely monitored. New in January 1950, this engine spent its first five months working from Darlington after delivery from NBL Co.. It then went to Stockton for eight years before returning to Darlington in June 1958. Withdrawn 13th September 1965, it was sold the following month for scrap.

Another ex works engine on Darlington shed that day was Q6 No.63411 which had just completed its last 'General', having been in works from 2nd April to 4th May. It was still 'running-in' and would have to go back into works on the 16th for a Non-Classified repair from which it would be released on the 23rd read to return to its home shed at Thornaby. In December 1962 it moved to Tyne Dock shed and was withdrawn from there on 6th April 1965. It was sold for scrap in June of that year to G.Cohen at Cargo Fleet. From new in 1919, this engine went first to Carlisle London Road shed for a twenty year stint before moving over to West Hartlepool in March 1939. At the outbreak of war it moved to Stockton and in April 1940 went back to West Hartlepool. Six weeks later on 18th May 1940 it went south to Springhead and stayed there until March 1943 when it was allocated to Neville Hill. Just three months later it was back on Teesside, at Haverton Hill shed. Then, in October 1944, it moved the short distance to Newport where it took up residence for four years. Its first reallocation under BR was to Middlesbrough where it worked from for nearly ten years until the shed was closed and it went to the newly opened shed at Thornaby.

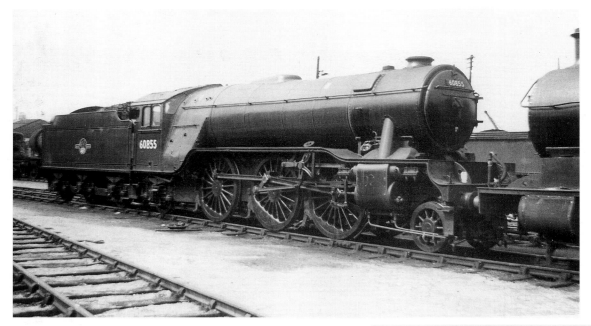

In the works yard York based V2 No.60855 was undergoing a Non-Classified repair after it had completed its last 'General' on 25th April. That repair had started on 12th March and culminated with a Smith type speedometer being fitted besides a fresh boiler. Obviously something wasn't quite right with the engine because it re-entered works on the 11th May. On the 17th it left but was back in on the 25th May again. That N/C repair lasted until 5th June after which it returned home. Its next visit to Darlington works, on 19th May 1964, was its last because it had come in for cutting up after being condemned on 13th April. Built at Darlington and released to traffic on 21st April 1939, the engine was twenty-five years and one month old when it returned for dismantling. Many of those years had been spent working the ECML first from King's Cross shed and from July 1940 New England shed. In November 1953 it returned to King's Cross. In the late summer of 1955 it had a near three month spell on the GC main line working from Neasden shed and after which it went back to King's Cross. On 20th October 1957 the GC beckoned once again and Neasden was its home for the next year until it moved for the last time, now to York in November 1958.

Like Doncaster, Grantham and York, Darlington station in steam days always had a main line pilot or stand-by engine available to cover any locomotive failures on the ECML express passenger trains. Usually these would consist a Pacific type and Darlington nearly always had an A3 on stand-by. On 13th May 1962 Darlington's A3 No.60091 CAPTAIN CUTTLE was on this duty and, as was usual for this particular job, the shed had turned out the A3 in a very presentable manner. Note the express headlamps already in place to save vital minutes in the event of a possible failure. No.60091 had been allocated to Darlington shed since the previous December having been at Gateshead for a year before that. In the June following this photograph, the Pacific returned to Tyneside, first to Gateshead shed and then in September to Heaton. In June 1963 it went back to Gateshead from where it worked until withdrawal on 12th October 1964. By the end of that year it had been purchased for scrap by Draper's in Hull and its fate was sealed. The trough or German type smoke deflectors had been fitted at Doncaster works during the engine's last General overhaul which took place during August, September and October 1961. This A3 spent some twenty years of its life working expresses over the Waverley route and was allocated to Canal shed in Carlisle from 26th October 1928 to 30th May 1948 when it moved to Gateshead shed and started a long association with the north-east.

J21 No.65033 stored inside the closed Darlington engine shed 23rd July 1967. The life of 65033 was not only long but was also interesting in the fact that *twice* it was reprieved from being scrapped. Built at Gateshead works in March 1889, it was shedded at West Hartlepool by Grouping with thirteen of its compatriots. In December 1936 it was sent south to Hull where it took up residency at Dairycoates shed until moving to Neville Hill in March 1943. However, during the interim period, in November 1939 it had been taken out of stock for scrapping only to be reinstated at the end of December because of the wartime emergency. A year after the end of the war, and still going strong, it moved back to the north-east and after a General overhaul it was allocated to Darlington shed in May 1946. From 17th November 1951 until 14th September 1952 it was outstationed at Reedsmouth shed. After that it began an on/off relationship with South Blyth shed and its first parting from that place took it to Hexham in November 1955. By the end of August 1958 it was back at Blyth until January of the following year when it moved to Blaydon. On 1st May 1960 it returned to South Blyth only to leave in mid January 1961 for Heaton shed. By the beginning of April it was once again, and for the final time, earning its keep at South Blyth. Its last General repair had taken place during 1956 but to enable it to haul a railtour in May 1960 it had been called into works for a repaint only on the 5th of that month. Life for the ancient 0-6-0 was seemingly going on forever but alas time catches up with everything, apparently, and on 23rd April 1962 No.65033 was condemned. With a view to preserving an example of the J21 class, and what better example than the oldest of them, 65033 was laid aside, in the open, at Darlington works. With it was sister engine No.65099 which was to be used as a source of spares in the event of preservation taking place. Once again, however, time was ticking ever onwards and with no decision having been made and the closure of Darlington works being imminent, No.65099 was sold for scrap. With its demise looking ever closer, No.65033 was moved off the closed works site to the engine shed at Bank Top whilst decisions were still being made. Eventually, just as its eightieth birthday was looming, the J21 was saved and can be seen today at the Beamish Open Air Museum. Bank Top engine shed, at the time this picture was taken, was being used as an overflow for diesel multiple units from the depot on the opposite of the main line.

On 23rd July 1967 I witnessed A4 No.4498 SIR NIGEL GRESLEY working a special northwards along the ECML through Durham and in this view the preserved engine has just started to cross the viaduct south of the station. Another of the fascinations of railways' to me, besides steam locomotives, is the landscape surrounding the course of the various lines. Here, at the south end of the viaduct, the hillside brings the scale of man's engineering achievements into perspective. The lofty viaduct dwarfs not just the train crossing it but also the infrastructure of the town around and below it. From a modelling point of view this is lovely stuff with apparently no two buildings the same and all on differing levels. Finally, from a nostalgic point of view, just look at that corner shop - those were the days.

From the same vantage point I caught the A4 passing through Durham station on the Down fast, en route to Newcastle. There appears to be enough coal in tender and water was not a problem at this time as some of the troughs on the ECML were still and situ and operational - just. This was the heart of the Durham Coalfield although little evidence of the industry can be seen. Although in decline, compared with the production rich days of the first quarter of this century, during the summer of 1967 there was still sixty-six collieries winding coal in the county and many of those were within a few miles of Durham city centre. The names given to the 'pits' do not give any clues as to the toil, and sometimes the suffering which was an everyday part of winning the coal. A selection of those collieries Vested into the NCB in 1947 include Adventure; Bearpark; Dean & Chapter; East Hedley Hope; Eden; Hole-in-the-wall; Stargate; Twizell Burn Drift, to name but a few. On a lighter note perhaps, the prison, part of which can be seen on the right, was undergoing expansion.

Approaching the junction of the main line and dock line (Newburn Jct.) at West Hartlepool in July 1967, Q6 No.63344 is heading for the docks with a coal train. This view from Newburn bridge is looking northwards and on the left is the motive power depot which was amongst the last engine sheds on the North Eastern Region to close to steam. Between the juncture of the two routes can be seen the former wagon shop which had been closed for some years but as can be seen was still very much intact. The Q6 had come to West Hartlepool from Tyne Dock shed in the previous October and was withdrawn in September, being sold the following month for scrap to T.J.Thompson at Stockton.

Looking in the opposite direction from Newburn bridge, which carried the A178 road over the railway, we can see Seaton Carew in the distance. On the east side of the main line the Newburn yards stretch for about a mile, whilst on the west side of the line the large steelworks of the South Durham Steel & Iron Co. occupied much of the land over the same stretch as the railway sidings. Working its way south, with empty hoppers from the docks on 22nd April 1967, is Q6 No.63407 another West Hartlepool resident living on borrowed time. Built at Darlington in 1919, as NER No.2250, this engine had spent all of its life working from sheds in County Durham and Yorkshire. Dairycoates had its services first and then, in March 1940, it went to Cudworth, moving on to Neville Hill in March 1943. Under BR it moved north to Haverton Hill in 1949 and ten years later to West Auckland for a five year spell before moving to Darlington in February 1964 and then West Hartlepool two months later. Condemned in July, No.63407 was sold for scrap in September to Clayton & Davie of Dunston on Tyne.

(opposite) Late on Thursday morning 20th July 1967 I caught WD No.90382 heading northwards through Newburn Junction at West Hartlepool with a train on empty hoppers probably bound for Horden Colliery. The South Durham Steel & Iron works, the numerous chimneys of which dominate the skyline on the right of the picture, consumed vast quantities of coal and coke each day and it was this traffic and the end products of the iron and steel making which kept West Hartlepool shed so busy. Coal was brought from Blackhall, Easington and Horden collieries, which between them produced about three million tons of coal a year during the 1960's. Horden also processed in excess of 350,000 tons of coke a year. The engine shed (51C) stands on the right with withdrawn WD No.90309 waiting its turn to be towed away to become scrap to feed the local blast furnaces. In the foreground the weed strewn patch of land was once the yard of the wagon repair shop.

Continuing its journey northwards, 90382 passes the yard which separated the two engine sheds at West Hartlepool. The background is dominated by council maisonettes whilst the middle ground contains elevated tanks which from left to right are; two diesel fuel tanks. A large steel sided water tank erected on six tubular legs during the 1950's to supplement the depot water supply. The original brick built water tower topped by an iron segmented tank, and finally the water softening plant erected by the LNER to purify the locomotive water supply. On the far right is the original three road shed which was still in use. No.90382 was at this time a Sunderland South Dock engine which managed to work until the last day of steam on the NE Region.

No sooner had one WD passed through than another came cluncking by with a heavy coal train. The weather suddenly turned cloudy with patchy sunshine. No.90677 was a new arrival at West Hartlepool having left Hull Dairycoates in June for its last home. It too was to 'soldier on' until September.

Another midday foray to West Hartlepool on Monday 17th July 1967 found the weather behaving and bathing Ivatt mogul No.43070 which was making its way past the shed yard to pick up a train from Newburn yard. The 2-6-0 had a fully lined tender which, by this time in the 60's when plain black livery was the norm, was something of a rarity. This Darlington built engine had spent all of its life working from sheds within the North Eastern Region going, when new, to Heaton in August 1950. After seven years it moved south to Holbeck for eighteen months, then on to Bradford Hammerton Street before moving to York in October 1959. Thornaby had it from February 1961 until July 1962 when it went south again but this time to Wakefield. In January 1964 it went to Low Moor and exactly a year later to Ardsley. Back to Wakefield in October 1965, it came north to West Hartlepool in February 1967. At the end of the month when this picture was taken it transferred yet again, this time to its last shed at North Blyth from where in September it was withdrawn. In November it was sold for scrap to Clayton & Davie at Dunston on Tyne. On the shed yard can be seen one of the BR Sulzer Type 2 Bo-Bo diesel locomotives replenishing its fuel tanks. Note the brake tender, a device which was attached to many of the diesel locomotives in the region for added braking power when working one the numerous unfitted mineral trains still prevalent during this period.

The motive power depot at West Hartlepool consisted of two roundhouses built in the square style latterly adopted by the North Eastern Railway. To complement them a three road through shed stood at the northern end of the yard. The NER square roundhouse design could be found all over the former system and usually offered twenty-four stabling stalls around each turntable. Outside the twin roundhouse at West Hartlepool, at its north end, on Saturday 22nd April 1967 stood WD No.90339 and K1 No.62048, both in steam but leading a somewhat tenuous existence with condemnation just around the corner. The 2-8-0 had spent much of its life at Wakefield before moving to 51C in September 1966. Withdrawal took place in July 1967. The K1 had spent three stints at Darlington shed, the first time for just over a year from new in October 1949, then again from January to September 1951 when it moved to Haverton Hill for five years. Its last move to Darlington was in November 1959 and it was resident to closure of the shed when it transferred to West Hartlepool. In between the Darlington years it was at Heaton from November 1950 to January 1951 and York from June 1956 to November 1959. No.62048 was condemned 19th June 1967 and purchased for scrap by Garnham, Harris & Elton at Chesterfield in August 1967. The roundhouse shed faired no better than the engines it housed once the end of steam came in September 1967. Although diesel locomotives used the shed for a short while, the building was eventually demolished.

Considering it was a Saturday, the 22nd April 1967 was fairly quiet inside the two roundhouses at West Hartlepool engine shed and only a few occupants were stabled including these two 0-6-0 diesel mechanical shunters flanking Q6 No.63394. The 0-8-0 was a Darlington product of 1918 and was appropriately stood on a road with one of the original trumpet shaped smoke ventilators above. No.63394 had come to West Hartlepool in May 1965 from Consett but it was no newcomer to the depot having been resident here from March 1945, ex Darlington, to October 1947 when it went to Blaydon for a sixteen year stint prior to moving on to Percy Main in 1963 and then onto Consett in January 1964. Its longest stay at any shed was at Newport from May 1924 until February 1943 when it transferred to Darlington. Withdrawal was only weeks away from the time of this photograph and it was sold for scrap in August to Hughes, Bolckow at Blyth. The diesel mechanical's lasted a bit longer and at one time 51C had about a dozen of these lightweight shunting engines on its books. The first lot came in 1953 from Vulcan Foundry numbered D2204 to D2206. These were followed by Doncaster and Swindon built examples up to 1960. In 1959 another type introduced to the shed were seven Hunslet locomotives numbered D2586 to D2592. Both types found work in the various yards and docks around Hartlepool but the decreasing traffic and the mechanical breakdowns suffered by the Hunslet built 0-6-0DM's saw them gradually moved on. Ironically the four Hunslet engines still resident at the depot in March 1967 were all withdrawn and then sold for scrap, outlived by the likes of this near fifty year old Q6. This roundhouse shed was much older than that, the first of the twin sheds being erected in 1871 with the second one opening for business four years later. Both had different diameter turntables the first shed had a 50ft example whilst the newer shed had a 42ft table. At first they were completely covered by boards, however, over the years the covering had disappeared for one reason or another and their pits were open, a hazard to the unwary. Each shed was also equipped with a set of hydraulic iron framed sheerlegs.

Further up the yard at West Hartlepool, at the north end, stood the older 1867 built shed, a three road structure with through roads. This view on the 17th July 1967 shows the dilapidated roof and smoke vents - the time for demolition was not far away. Two WD's and a Q6 are visible, the numbers of the 2-8-0s were 90061 and 90385, the Q6 number is lost in my notes of the time. Both WD's were withdrawn and awaiting orders for movement to breakers yards. Note the air of dereliction about the place, such a common sight in the mid 1960's.

Three days later and the same aspect reveals 'just withdrawn' Q6 No.63407 has joined the two WD's, No.90061 having been pushed into the shed to make room for the 0-8-0.

On 22nd April 1967 the shed yard was still busy and one had to be careful when moving about the place. Here WD No.90482, one of those purchased by the LNER before its demise, makes its way off the shed yard and has the shunters pole traditionally (on the NE Region at least) jammed into one of the frame lifting holes. This engine had arrived at West Hartlepool in September 1966 from Wakefield, a shed which seems to have had all the NE Region WD's and others too, shedded there at one time or another. Built by Vulcan Foundry in 1944, this Austerity had gone first to Newport, then in April 1947 to Heaton. Tyne Dock welcomed it in November 1948 and in September 1951 Hull Dairycoates started a long association with it which lasted until July 1964. During that time it moved to the neighbouring ex Hull & Barnsley shed at Springhead from December 1956 to November 1958. The WD 2-8-0s were something of a godsend for the LNER and British Railways, filling a vital need for heavy freight locomotives which, seemingly, were easy to maintain. They could slog their way through the day and were usually kept in a diabolical external condition. Why a BR version of this seven hundred and thirty-three strong class was never preserved is a mystery but they went as they came - in great numbers over a short space of time.

Ivatt Class 4MT No.43070 has the breakdown train duty on 22nd April 1967. The West Hartlepool breakdown train consisted a hotchpotch of vans and old coaching stock equipped with all sorts of gear for rerailing grounded vehicles. Always on call, and used on a regular basis, this train would attend incidents wherever it was required. Its usual sphere of operations was along the coast line south to Billingham, northwards to Seaham and along the lines inland as far west as the ECML. Breakdown cranes, if required were available from either Thornaby or Gateshead depots.

Peppercorn K1 No.62041 had spent all of its short life, from leaving the North British Locomotive Co.'s Queen's Park works in October 1949, working in the south-east Durham area, first, for a few months from Darlington shed where its running-in progress was checked and then, from February 1950 and for the greater part of its life, from Stockton shed. It transferred to Thornaby for a few weeks in June 1959 before returning to Darlington for a seven year stay. On the closure of Darlington depot in March 1966 it went to West Hartlepool to work out the last year of its operational life. With a glut of serviceable steam locomotives during this period of the sixties', sheds were condemning engines for the slightest problem which might require a works visit and the fact that none of BR's workshops were carrying out steam locomotive repairs anyway 'the writing was on the wall'. So in April 1967 No.62041's number came up for whatever reason. On 13th July scrap merchant Arnott Young purchased the K1 along with sister 62026 and WD 90309. When I photographed 62041 at the rear of the West Hartlepool coaling stage on Monday 17th July 1967, it was ready and prepared for its short one-way journey to Dinsdale and oblivion.

(opposite) K1 No.62026 and WD No.90309 stand silently at the rear of the West Hartlepool coaling stage in company with 62041 whose tender is just visible on the right. this K1 had only arrived at West Hartlepool on 28th May and was withdrawn in July. Note the amount of coal in the tender which appears to have been topped up prior to failure. Whether or not the engine travelled to Dinsdale with its full tender is unknown but with a lack of available staff to remove seven and a half tons of coal at the BR depot, the scrap merchant probably got a little 'windfall'. No.62026 was also turned out by the NBL Co. in 1949 and it was sent, like many others of its class, to Blaydon shed until May 1962 when it moved to Gateshead for a nearly three year stay. Sunderland beckoned in February 1965, Tyne Dock in October 1966, then North Blyth found some use for it on their numerous coal trips from January 1967. On 14th May it returned to Sunderland for a couple of weeks before going to its last shed. Typical of the period, much of the remaining work was being taken by the growing fleet of diesel locomotives and serviceable steam engines were flitting about from shed to shed. WD 90309 was another 'orphan' from the closing of Darlington shed and it too had been withdrawn in the July of my visit. Note that its tender is also reasonably full - another 'windfall'? The coaling stage at West Hartlepool, with its ramp entering from the north end of the yard, was sited nearer to the twin roundhouses than the through shed but served both establishments. Neither the LNER nor BR saw any reason to modernise the servicing facilities at this depot and they remained much as the NER intended until closure on 17th September 1967.

With just enough coal in its tender to enable it to complete its next duty, WD No.90695 makes its way towards Newburn Junction to pick up empty coal hoppers for return to one of the coastal collieries north of Hartlepool on Monday 17th July 1967. This engine was a recent acquisition for West Hartlepool shed, its last shed, Dairycoates having sent it, complete with grime in June. No.90695 was given a painted-on version of the 51C shedplate by the shed staff and the engine would go on until the end of steam on the NE Region, being withdrawn on the 17th September 1967 for no other reason than it was "no longer required".

Later in the day Austerity No.90695 came clanking under the NER elevated overline signal box and through West Hartlepool station with its train of empties in tow. The curve which the engine has just negotiated has brought it from a south/north to an east/west direction but once through the platforms the line once again takes on a south/north course until the coast north of Hartlepool is reached and then a north-westerly direction is attained. In the left background a part of the extensive docks can be seen with piles of imported timber lining the quays. Today the port is still active though nothing like it was in the 1960s and some of the sheltered docks have become marinas for the yacht owning fraternity. Shipbreaking is still carried out here, as recorded by the recent controversial acquisition of some ex United States Navy Reserve vessels for scrap. Back in the 60s, when steam motive power was still very much in business, nobody cared much about environmental issues and everyone just got on with what was necessary, no matter if it was dirty, exhausting, unsavoury or otherwise. Note the crossed shunters' poles now adorning the front of the WD - Shunters - now there was a dodgy job if ever there was one.

At the other (western) end of West Hartlepool station (by this time "West" had been painted out on all signs to read just "Hartlepool") the curve, as explained in the previous caption, took on a northerly direction again, forming a huge letter 'S'. WD No.90009 was in little danger of derailment through excessive speed as it drifted through the platforms on 20th July 1967. This was a Sunderland engine and another recent acquisition from Hull Dairycoates when that shed closed on 24th June. The engine has not yet been fitted with a shed plate and probably never was before its September withdrawal. Built 1943 by the NBL Co., as WD No.77336, it was renumbered 3009 in February 1947 and then 63009 in March 1948. It became 90009 in October 1950. When the LNER purchased the engine it was sent to Woodford shed in March 1946, then on to Gorton five months later. Mexborough got it in April 1947 and then Springhead in August 1948. Dairycoates was its next shed and it arrived there in February 1949 and in the following September York borrowed it for four months before handing it back in time for Christmas and the start of an eighteen year residency. It was cut up in Blyth by Hughes, Bolckow. Note the high water towers at the end of the platform, yet another common sight around the railway system in this particular area of County Durham.

We saw WD No.90009 rounding the curve at West Hartlepool opposite and on the previous day also. Today, on the 19th, the Austerity has charge of a train of empties at Ryhope and is headed for Vane Tempest Colliery. The train has just passed Ryhope Grange Junction and is on the former Londonderry line from Sunderland South Dock to Seaham and Hartlepool. The line seen on the left at this point is the Seaton Bank line (ex Durham & Sunderland) to Stockton and of course many more collieries on the way. On the skyline, above the train, can be seen Sunderland itself and the home of this 2-8-0 for a few more months anyway. Today, between Ryhope Grange and South Dock, the Londonderry lines have been lifted and the Durham & Sunderland line singled.

(opposite) Heading south on the Stockton route on 19th July 1967, J27 No.65882 has charge of a train of empty hoppers bound for Silksworth Colliery, one of the numerous pits in this part of County Durham still working. Up ahead is the junction and signal box for the Silksworth branch (the bracket signal for which can be seen indicating a clear road) which had two productive collieries along its short length up to 1966 when Ryhope Colliery was closed with the loss more than a thousand jobs. The other pit on the branch, Silksworth Colliery, which opened in 1878 was still producing more than 400,000 tons of saleable coal a year but by 1971 that mine too would be closed. A much more recent colliery was Vane Tempest which can be seen on the horizon in front of the locomotive. That mine, opened in 1928, was producing about one million tons of coal a year up to 1992 when it was also abandoned. No.65882 was not as old as the branch but had some years over Vane Tempest pit. The J27 had spent much of its life hauling Durham coal but not all of it as is revealed by its allocation history. Built at Darlington on the eve of Grouping, its first shed was Shildon then in November 1926 it moved down to March and enjoyed nine years of employment in the Fens. In December 1935 it was moved to Langwith Junction shed and was again hauling coal trains from the pitheads for a living. One month after the outbreak of World War Two it went to Grantham shed and in June 1940 went back to North Eastern territory, shedded at York until March 1943 when the 'class concentrations' saw it allocated to Selby shed. After eleven years of moving Yorkshire coal it went to Heaton in May 1954 and then in July 1959 to North Blyth, hauling Northumberland coal. In September 1962 Heaton got it back but only until the following June when it went to Sunderland for three months, moving to South Blyth in September. Its final move came in April 1967 when it returned to Sunderland and Durham coal. It was condemned on 9th September 1967 and one month later was in the hands of Stockton scrap merchant T.J.Thompson; no doubt having traversed this route one last time to get there.

This view of 65882 at Ryhope on the 20th July 1967 shows just a half of the train of empty hoppers it was hauling on this glorious summer afternoon, making its way to Silksworth. This particular photograph was got from a farmer's field, with his blessing. Indeed, it was as though the farmer himself knew that the last couple of months of steam working in the north-east had to be recorded on film and so he was very obliging in letting me cross the field on a sort of unofficial footpath mainly for his use. Of course every courtesy was given and I have found over the years that it pays dividends to be both civil and polite no matter which way the permission goes.

My final shot at Ryhope in 1967 has Tyne Dock based Peppercorn K1 No.62011 heading towards Sunderland with this loaded coal train during the early evening of 20th July. With steam shut off, the mogul is virtually drifting along the line with the heavy load of power station coal held in check. On the Up line another train of empties is pegged and just after the K1 had passed a WD came trundling through, clanking away in that distinctive sound that only WD 2-8-0s seemed to make. No.62011 had spent most of its life working on the old North British section of Scotland. New from NBL Co. in 1949, it went first to Gorton and then in May 1950 to March. However, in February 1952 it took the long journey north to Glasgow and for four months was a Eastfield shed. In the June it went to Fort William and stayed for ten years before being ousted by dieselisation of the West Highland line in December 1962. Luckily the North Eastern Region still needed steam motive power so it moved to Alnmouth in that cold winter of 1962. Closure of Alnmouth shed in June 1966 saw it move on the South Blyth where its usefulness was used until the following October when it 'crossed the river' to North Blyth. In March 1967 its final move took it to Tyne Dock shed and when the end came on 9th September it was sold to Hughes, Bolckow and went back to Blyth for scrapping in December 1967, having just reached middle age in locomotive terms.

(*opposite*) Approximately halfway between Sunderland South Dock and Ryhope, on the coast line south of Sunderland, is Grangetown level crossing. In July 1967 there was still plenty of steam locomotives active and working the coal trains to and from the collieries to the docks and other customers in the north-east. The crossing was an excellent place to watch and photograph the procession of empties and fulls toing and froing along the line. It is hard to believe now but at that time in the summer of 67, steam motive power would be finished with just two months away. Seen the previous day at Monkwearmouth, entering the Wearmouth Colliery line with a train of empties, J27 No.65879 keeps a loaded coal train, from a different colliery, in check at its heads north towards Sunderland on the 18th July.

Sunderland South Dock shed on 2nd April 1967 was like the last refuge of orphan NE Region steam. WD's galore with J27's, Q6's and a few K1's, had gathered to work their last days. Most were in urgent need of a clean and many required maintenance which was sadly lacking. Those that fell by the wayside were condemned and put up for sale. WD No.90056 was about to become one of the fallen and although in steam during my visit, it was just nine days away from being condemned. It had arrived at Sunderland in December 1966 after an eight year stay in the West Riding, spending much of its time at Wakefield shed. It returned to Yorkshire once again being cut up by Draper's at their yard in Hull on Monday 7th August 1967. The depot at South Dock comprised of two buildings, a four road straight shed which had its origins back to 1857, although BR had rebuilt the place in 1954. The other shed was a roundhouse opened in 1875 and operational up to the end of steam on 17th September 1967 after which it was demolished. Diesel locomotives used the straight shed for stabling until about 1988 when dwindling traffic saw them move on with the shed falling into disrepair and eventual demolition.

(opposite) Occupants of the roundhouse at Sunderland on 22nd April 1967 included these two J27's Nos.65817 and 65894. The former was another of the May 1908 built engines from NBL Co., which started its working life at Percy Main spending thirty-two years there. In January 1940 it went to West Hartlepool for just over four years which included an eight week loan to Northallerton in early 1944. Borough Gardens got it in May 1944 until April 1947 when Sunderland acquired it for the first time. In February 1964 it went to Thornaby and on 5th October that year it was condemned only to be returned to traffic five days later and the very next day was transferred back to Percy Main. At the end of November 1964 it entered Darlington works for a 'Heavy Intermediate' overhaul which prolonged its working life for another two years. Leaving works on 16th January 1965 it went back to its home shed only to be reallocated to Sunderland when the North Tyneside shed was closed on 28th February 1965. It was withdrawn in May 1967 and sold for scrap during the following July to W.Willoughby at Choppington. No.65894's life was somewhat shorter by the fact that it was built fifteen years after its sister J27 and by the LNER at Darlington in September 1923, the last of the class. Its first shed was Ferryhill and in February 1930 it moved south to York. During World War Two it went to Neville Hill returning to York seven years later in February 1950. In its bid to rid itself of steam locomotives York sent the still useful 0-6-0 to Sunderland in October 1966 where it spent nearly twelve months working until withdrawn on 9th September 1967. It was sold for preservation to the NELPG on 28th November of that same year.

Q6 No.63395 was one of the lucky ones although in this 22nd April 1967 view at Sunderland shed it looks anything but looked after. The engine was still in traffic and evidently had been engaged on some late season snow clearance duties around the area, with a miniature plough which was probably performing its last ever work. Arriving at Sunderland in May 1965 from Darlington shed, the Q6 went into Darlington works later that year and received a 'Heavy Intermediate' overhaul which actually put it in fine fettle to be a candidate for preservation and indeed, after withdrawal on 9th September 1967, it was purchased for such on 29th October 1967 and is now working at the NYMR. Before its 'afterlife' No.63395 started work at Blaydon shed in December 1918, numbered 2238. After twenty-five years it moved down to Newport in 1943 and then to Darlington shortly afterwards. By the end of the war it was resident in West Hartlepool where it stayed through the latter years of the LNER. In September 1949 it went south to Dairycoates then later that year to Selby where it enjoyed ten years of working on the relatively flat land found in the area before moving back north to Darlington.

WD No.90135 (although it could be virtually any member of the class) leads J27 No.65811 north through Monkwearmouth on 18th July 1967, past the junction of the Wearmouth Colliery line. Both engines are in a deplorable external condition but at least they are operational. The J27 had spent all of its life, since being built in 1908, in the north-east and had moved to its last shed, Sunderland South Dock in April 1967 from North Blyth. Before reaching the north-east, the Austerity had been at the usual havens of the WD's in West Yorkshire at Mirfield, Ardsley and lastly Wakefield which it left in December 1966 to move to Sunderland South Dock. Both engines were running out the last weeks of their lives and were withdrawn en masse with the rest of the South Dock steam locomotive allocation on 9th September.

The Monkwearmouth district of Sunderland stood on the north bank of the River Wear with the main line to Newcastle passing right through its middle. Coal traffic in the area during the 1960s was still very important with dozens of collieries within a ten mile radius of Sunderland still producing millions of tons of coal each year. Monkwearmouth station in particular was a good place to observe the passing traffic with empties' and fulls' coming and going with no particular discernible pattern involved except for the traffic to and from the nearby Wearmouth Colliery. On Wednesday 19th July 1967, WD No.90378 crosses the Wear bridge and heads north through the station with a loaded coal train. This Sunderland South Dock engine was a new arrival on Wearside having been ousted from Dairycoates by dieselisation. It went on to end, being withdrawn on 17th September with all the other operational steam locomotives at South Dock shed.

A rear aspect of 90378 showing the usual build up of grime associated with these very able and durable locomotives. The old North Eastern footbridge - what a great place to watch trains from - is a superb example of cast iron design and craftsmanship, its graceful arch fulfilling everything asked of it. Today, in the relentless march of health and safety, such style has been lost to austere functionalism and cost savings.

On the previous day Peppercorn K1 No.62007, with a remarkably clean front end, came drifting through Monkwearmouth station with a train of empty hoppers from Tyne Commission Quay bound for one of the collieries south of Sunderland. No.62007 was at this time a Tyne Dock engine and had gone there in the previous October after a twelve month stint at Sunderland. Built in 1949 by the NBL Co., the mogul went to Darlington shed for a few months before going to Heaton for three years. Returning to Darlington for an eleven year residency in July 1952, the engine moved south to York in August 1963, then on to Neville Hill in June 1964. Its transfer to Sunderland took place in the October of the following year. Not quite lasting to the end, the K1 was withdrawn on 9th September and was sold for scrap the same month to Hughes, Bolckow at Blyth. The multi-storey building in the background constituted, I think, high rise flats, a typical 60's development. I wonder if T. Dan Smith had anything to do with that one?

(opposite) Earlier in the day J27 No.65879, another recent Sunderland acquisition, arrived from the south with a train of empty hoppers for Wearmouth Colliery. The 'pit' was also situated on the north bank of the Wear, just west of the main line, the tracks giving access ran between the small building and the wall at the left of the picture.

The 0-6-0 set its train back onto the Up main from where crossovers gave direct access to the colliery line. Here the J27 has just cleared the points and has stopped, ready to pull forward. Monkwearmouth station once had goods facilities on both sides of the main line but those on the east side had been taken out some years ago although relics still remained such as the load gauge. The signal box was obviously required here as so many movements would have taken place every day. Note how high the brick base lifts the box so that the bobby could see right over the adjacent road bridge, a distinct help in carrying out this particular manoeuvre. The colliery branch can just be seen in front of the white gabled building through the third arch of the bridge.

No.65879 gingerly makes its way onto the single line branch to Wearmouth Colliery. This J27 was amongst the last of the North Eastern 0-6-0s, being built in 1922 at Darlington. Its first shed was Neville Hill and from there it moved to Heaton in July 1924 then, two months later, it went further north to Tweedmouth. As if to become one of the most travelled members of its class, it then ventured onto former Great Eastern metals and was transferred to March shed in August 1926. After four years there, it went westwards to Peterborough East shed and, after three years at that place it moved across town to the ex Great Northern shed at New England. Fourteen months later, in a bid to get back into home territory, it got as far north as Ardsley before being recalled to Cambridge in September 1938. However, in March 1940 home beckoned and the 0-6-0 journeyed up to Tyneside for a three year stint at Blaydon shed. In March 1943 North Blyth managed to secure its services and did so until September 1956 when it moved to Heaton. One year later it returned to North Blyth for another nine years. In October 1966 it transferred to South Blyth shed and on 28th May 1967 it ended up at Sunderland South Dock shed, its near nomadic life nearly over. Condemned 9th September, it did not quite reach that fateful day of the 17th. The following month saw it sold for scrap to T.J.Thompson of Stockton and soon after it ceased to exist. Most of these useful and versatile engines had long lives from the pre-Group period through the LNER and into BR days, a tribute to their design and manufacture.

Tyne Dock engine shed closed on 9th September 1967, just one week before steam was banished in the Region. However, long before the end came the shed had the appearance of an engine graveyard with semi derelict buildings surrounding filthy, rusting locomotives which seemed to have been left to rot where they stood. One such engine which appeared to have these credentials was WD No.90370 of Sunderland South Dock shed, captured on film on the 16th July 1967 outside the south end of No.1 shed. Withdrawn in the previous May, the 2-8-0 had come from Wakefield in October 1966 and had probably been failed at Tyne Dock after working in from Sunderland. The engine facility at Tyne Dock had been established in 1862 when a roundhouse was built on the site of what was later converted to a straight shed with one through road, four stabling roads and a one road fitting shop. Another roundhouse, which became known as No.2 shed, was tacked onto the south side of this shed about 1871. In 1877 yet another roundhouse was built on the south end of that shed. This became No.3 shed and was equipped with a set of hydraulic sheerlegs. Both of these roundhouses had 42ft turntables. The final shed, latterly known as No.1 shed, was also a roundhouse and of slightly larger proportions to the previous buildings. This opened in the 1890's and had a 50ft turntable and two sets of iron framed hydraulic sheerlegs. The coal stage, built to the usual NER style with a ramp, was situated some distance from the shed towards the staiths. In latter years a 60ft turntable was installed in the yard outside No.1 shed.

(opposite) Accompanying the WD on the coal stack road of No.1 shed was Q6 No.63366. Also without any coupling or connecting rods and front numberplate and shed plate, the 0-8-0 was obviously another candidate for the scrapyard. It too had been withdrawn in May and was bound eventually for Drapers in Hull where it was cut up on 11th September 1967. A Tyne Dock engine since December 1962, this Q6 had spent all of its working days at sheds in County Durham since being built as NER No.1335 at Darlington in 1913. Borough Gardens shed was its first home then, in March 1943 it moved to Stockton and then nearby Newport in September 1944. During the second month of BR's existence it returned to Borough Gardens, this time for an eleven year stint. Blaydon got it in June 1959 before it moved down the Tyne to 52H.

Departmental J72 No.58, formerly No.69005 was in store at Tyne Dock shed on 16th July 1967 prior to withdrawal on the 7th October. built at Darlington in November 1949, this engine was amongst the last of a long line of one hundred and thirteen J72's built by the North Eastern, the LNER and British Railways, which had started with No.68670 (NER No.462) in December 1898 and finished with No.69028 in May 1951. No.69005 was allocated initially to Gateshead shed and was maintained by Gateshead works until its last repair, a 'General' in the winter of 1961-62 which was carried out at Darlington works. On 26th October 1964 it was transferred to North Blyth shed and renumbered 58 in the Departmental Stock. The reason for this two pronged move was to enable the coal shippers at the staiths in North Blyth to thaw the coal in the wagons received from collieries, using steam heating generated by the 0-6-0. J72 No.69023, renumbered 59, was also sent with 69005. During the summer months of 1965 they went into storage at Heaton shed. However, in the end the experiment was not successful and the winter of 1965/66 the two engines were moved to Gateshead shed, which was by now purely a diesel depot, where No.58 was used to supply steam for cleaning the bogies of diesel locomotives. That job too was not a success and Tyne Dock shed was then used to store the pair. No.59 was withdrawn September 1966 but faired better than No.58, being sold for preservation to a private individual in the same month. No.58 was sold for scrap in January 1968 to W.Willoughby at Choppington.

Why North Blyth based Ivatt 4MT No.43137 was receiving remedial attention at Tyne Dock on the 16th July 1967 is unknown but it was later put back into traffic and worked to closure of its home shed on 9th September. These hydraulic sheerlegs were 'inside' the roofless No.1 roundhouse and although the situation was far from ideal for engine repairs, it was excellent for photography. How long ago the roof of this shed had been removed I have no idea but it appears to have been some years since rain has helped cultivate the weeds which were growing all over the place. The 1951 Doncaster built mogul had started its career at South Lynn shed on the former Midland & Great Northern line but after less than a month there it was sent to Eastfield (exNBR) in Glasgow and after just over two years at that place it went further north to Mallaig (exNBR) but by July 1953 was back in Glasgow where it settled down for eight years before moving to Grangemouth (exCR) in March 1961. In September 1963 it ventured south again, this time to Wakefield (exLYR). Copley Hill (exGNR) had it from January to September 1964 went it returned to Wakefield. Ardsley (exGNR) had it during most of 1965 and in October of that year it went back to Wakefield. Perhaps the Yorkshire shed saw it as something of a bad penny but they kept hold of it until August 1966 when it went to its last shed at North Blyth (exNER). To say that it got amongst the old company sheds is an understatement.

Another sorry sight at Tyne Dock on Sunday 16th July 1967 was this withdrawn Q6 which was languishing in the corner of the yard between the fitting shop in the background, and the roofless No.1 shed on the right. No.63455 had been built by Armstrong Whitworth in 1920 as NER No.2298. Its first shed was Neville Hill where it had a twenty-three year stay until moving north to Consett in June 1943. After twenty-two years at that place it came down to the lowlands and Tyne Dock shed in May 1965. Withdrawal occurred in the June prior to my visit and it was sold for scrap in August to Garnham, Harris & Elton at Chesterfield. For this photograph I used the yard turntable as a vantage point.

On a previous visit to Tyne Dock, on 22nd April 1967, I found a little bit more locomotive activity but still lots of building dereliction. K1 No.62023 was active though being a Saturday it was having a rest from the chores of the previous week. The engine is stabled on the line alongside the fitting shop which can be seen on the right. The depot's water tank, with the cleaners' mess beneath is in the left background. By now the cleaners had all gone, either passed as firemen or had left for other occupations in the run down to closure of the shed. Note the 0-6-0 diesel mechanical shunter stabled outside the straight road shed. Diesels used the shed for stabling purposes until February 1970 when they too were sent elsewhere, the shed was completely demolished and housing then built on the site. The K1 had, since being built in 1949, always been allocated to a shed in the north-east with Blaydon being its first home. In May 1962 it went to Consett but within four months had moved to Heaton. Its stay there was even shorter and after less than two months it reallocated to Alnmouth where it settled in for a near four year spell. By June 1966 it had gone to Sunderland and on 23rd October came to Tyne Dock. Withdrawn on 26th June 1967, this was another North Eastern Region engine which ended up at a Chesterfield scrapyard, being sold in September. Note that none of the Tyne Dock engines carried shedplates.

Creeping through Newcastle Central station on Wednesday 26th July 1967, Sunderland based J27 No.65892, one of the latter and LNER Darlington built examples of that class, is less than two weeks away from condemnation. Its train consists of empty hoppers, no doubt en route to either a colliery or the Derwenthaugh coking plant. This engine spent all of its life in the north-east of England and up to withdrawal on 7th August 1967, after nearly forty-four years service, it had been allocated ten times to eight different sheds in either County Durham or Northumberland. It met its end at W.Willougby's scrapyard in Choppington during the winter of 1967. Note the former Western Region based diesel multiple unit in the background. These were used on the Newcastle - Whitley Bay circular just after the 3rd rail electric stock had finished on 17th June.

South Blyth engine shed consisted of a six road dead end building which had been built in two similar though slightly different styles. J27 No.65855 was stabled on No.3 road of the original three road shed. The first section of the shed was erected in 1880 just to the north of the running lines from the terminal station. The second part of the shed was opened fourteen years later, tacked onto the north wall of the original shed. The yard contained all the usual locomotive servicing facilities including coal stage, 50ft turntable and a sand furnace. By the early 1960s diesels had started to encroach on the shed and on my visit during Saturday 22nd April 1967 only a handful of steam engines were about the place. These included 65860 and 65861 sharing the place with 65855. This Beyer, Peacock built engine had come into traffic during 1908 and would have celebrated its 60th birthday if it had not been withdrawn on 9th September 1967. Starting its working life at Newport, it moved to Stockton in June 1935 and in January 1937 went to Haverton Hill. When that place closed in June 1959 it moved to the new depot at Thornaby. Just over four years later it was called to South Blyth and at the end of the May it went to its last shed - Sunderland. It was sold for scrap in October to T.J.Thompson and returned to Stockton for the last time.

Four months after my previous visit I returned to South Blyth on Saturday 15th July 1967 and found just one steam locomotive at the shed - 65813. This ghost like image is appropriate in the fact that the J27 had been withdrawn on 24th May and was awaiting a visit from local scrap metal merchants Hughes, Bolckow who purchased it in August. This engine was a North British Loco. Co. built J27 and also came into traffic during 1908 at Percy Main where it served until that depot closed to steam in February 1965. BR obviously saw some life still left in the fifty-seven year old engine and sent it to South Blyth shed for further work even though its last 'General' had taken place five years previously. On 9th January the following year it went to North Blyth but they sent it back to South Blyth on 23rd October but most work by now was being taken over by diesels and so its fate was sealed. This view is taken on No.1 road, inside the older portion of the shed; the sand furnace is through the archway on the right. South Blyth engine shed closed to steam on 28th May 1967 and to diesel locomotives on 29th January 1968.

The most northerly of the sheds visited in the July of 1967 was North Blyth and here on the 24th, at the throat of the shed, I photographed Ivatt Cl.4 No.43063 and the Packing van of the depot's breakdown train passing the signal box which carried the same name as the shed. In the distance can be seen part of the engine shed and its yard with a couple of diesel mechanical shunters visible. Beyond them a line of stored and withdrawn steam locomotives stretches towards the terraced houses backing onto the shed. To the right of the shed, elevated slightly in relation to the yard, can be seen the sidings serving the coal staiths built on this bank of the river and which are off picture to the far right. This signal box controlled the coming and going from those sidings which turned out onto this junction and the start of the main line to Cambois. Immediately behind the signal box was the National Coal Board independent line to their own staiths situated at the most southerly point on this part of the headland.

On 15th July I visited North Blyth shed and was struck first by the fact that most of the engines in steam appeared to be these Ivatt 2-6-0s. Not only were these engines veering towards the ugly side of the good looks spectrum, they were also in a deplorable external condition. It was obvious that these locomotives were only here as a stop gap until steam was banished from the Region for good. In the meantime the local enginemen put up with them and got the best out of them. Although only seventeen or so years old, these moguls, like the rest of the steam locomotive fleet at that time, were in many cases seriously run down and worn out - the old toys were discarded in favour of the new. Except for a twelve month period during 1966 and 1967, Doncaster built No.43050 had spent all of its short working life in the north-east of England. Its first shed in July 1950 was Darlington, quickly followed by Middlesbrough a couple of months later. It was nearly six years before it changed sheds again and then it was only down the road to Haverton Hill in May 1956. Four months later 43050 was back at Darlington shed and this time it was there for almost ten years before moving across to West Hartlepool in March 1966. A month later it moved out of the area altogether and went to Bradford for a twelve month stint at Manningham shed (note the 55F crudely painted on the smokebox door where a shed plate of sorts should be). Wakefield got it for a few weeks in April 1967 and then it returned home to the north-east and to North Blyth. Withdrawal was just days away when this picture was taken with class leader No.43000. Built at Horwich in 1947, this 2-6-0 was a true LMS engine and had started its working life at the southern end of that system at Bletchley after a tour of various establishments showing off its new design. In December 1950 it went to Devons Road shed in Bow and stayed until October 1957 when that shed went through a modernisation ready to become the first 'diesel only' shed on BR. Moving to Nuneaton, it worked from there until April 1961 went it took a big leap northwards to Carlisle Upperby. Eighteen months later it changed allegiance and went across the city to the former North British shed at Canal but was back on ex LMS property in June 1963. Its final move brought it to North Blyth in August 1966. It lasted until the end of steam in September 1967. By November, just twenty years old, it was in the hands of scrap merchants Clayton & Davie at Dunston along with No.43050.

The engine shed at North Blyth consisted a single square roundhouse equipped from the outset with twenty-four stabling roads. Opened for business in 1897, it housed locomotives engaged solely with the movement of coal from the pits to the staiths built out into the river. Closed on 9th September 1967, it was soon afterwards demolished when a new diesel depot was opened at Cambois. Inside the shed on Saturday 15th July 1967 was Peppercorn K1 No.62027 which had been condemned in March and had just been bought for scrap by Arnott Young. This was the K1's third shed, having arrived from Consett in late May 1965. Prior to May 1962 it had worked, like so many others of the class when new, from Blaydon shed. Of the two Ivatt's, No.43063 was still operational and would be to the end in a few months time whilst No.43055 had just been condemned and was awaiting a buyer. We has seen 43055 earlier when it was working from York shed and there it little more to be told of its life. However, 43063 which had a circuitous journey to end up here is worth looking at as it started life at New England shed in November 1950 being one of the Doncaster batch built that year. In June 1956 it moved to Woodford Halse for a six year stay and then in March 1962 it went to Saltley. By September of that year it was resident at Heaton Mersey shed and worked from there until August 1966 when it arrived at North Blyth. Like the class leader and 43050, No.43063 ended its days in the hands of Clayton & Davie.

Another of North Blyth's discarded Ivatt moguls on 15th July 1967 was No.43101, dumped on the through road from the roundhouse where it entered what could be termed 'the back yard'. The engine was immediately behind K1 No.62027 and had been withdrawn at the same time, in the previous March. This engine was destined to go to the 'local' Arnott Young scrapyard at Dinsdale in December but during its sixteen year working life the engine certainly got around the North Eastern Region. Darlington built, No.43101 went with a number of its kind to Dairycoates in February 1951. Just over a year later it moved to Middlesbrough and three and a half years later went to Kirkby Stephen but only for seven month stint, after which it went to Gateshead in June 1956 rubbing shoulders with the aristocrats of the steam locomotive world. That stay was also short lived and in November it crossed the Tyne to Heaton. In June 1957 a more radical move took place and it started a relationship with the engine sheds of the West Riding, first at Ardsley and three months later at Low Moor. In June 1958 it returned to Ardsley for a year before going on to Wakefield. In February 1961 Thornaby called and used the 2-6-0 for eighteen months before diesels took its work and it went south yet again, returning to Wakefield. In January 1964 Copley Hill was a surprising home for eight months prior to another year long stint at Ardsley. By October 1965 it was at its final shed, used until it was no longer mechanically sound.

This ten locomotive line-up of withdrawn engines in the yard of North Blyth shed on the 25th July 1967 comprised the following types from left to right; three Ivatt Cl.4's, the first two numbered 43117 and 43123; one Peppercorn K1; three J27's, 65861, 65885 and one unidentified; one Ivatt Cl.4; another K1 and finally another Ivatt Cl.4. The smokebox numberplates had been removed from all the engines as had the few shed plates. No doubt the various scrap merchants of the period had their favourite types for whatever reasons because the two Ivatt moguls heading this procession went to Clayton & Davie whilst the J27's went to Hughes, Bolckow. All were purchased at about the same time so perhaps price, metal content or even cost of haulage and distance had a bearing on who bought what. One thing was for certain - there were no preserved engines in this lot, no last minute reprieves. They were viewed for what they were - scrap metal.

A final look at one of the condemned Ivatt's in the North Blyth shed yard. Withdrawn during the week of my visit to the area, No.43123 had spent the whole of its life working the North Eastern Region and had a some point managed to pick up a NER type exJ27 whistle. Built at Horwich, its first shed was Selby in August 1951. Eight years later it moved to Dairycoates and in July 1961 to West Hartlepool. In a reversal of the usual trend of these engines to gravitate northwards to Blyth, 43123 actually went south in April 1966 to York. Perhaps it was an April Fool joke that went wrong because York did not really require its services and it was probably lucky to escape withdrawal whilst at 50A. By October it was allocated to North Blyth and until July of the following year worked the coal trains on the short runs from pit to staith. In the left background can be seen a section of the battered and decrepit coal stage, its cladding long since given up any protection for the coalmen working inside. At a higher elevation are the sidings containing the hundreds of hopper wagons used to transport the coal to the Blyth staiths. They too are now long gone, along with the industry which, for over a century, put Blyth and the Northumberland coal field on the map.

Further along the line of withdrawn engines at North Blyth on 25th July 1967 were these three J27's. No.65861 is having the coal removed from its tender. The tarpaulin sheet, fitted to the cab roof to give a modicum of protection when running tender first, it slung out of the way in an untidy fashion. Dominating the background, between the engine shed and the housing terrace, can be seen the former North Eastern Railway staiths. This massive structure was built entirely of timber and was one of dozens built at the numerous east coast ports to enable the quick and easy loading of coal from the hopper wagon straight into ship's holds or bunkers. The staiths relied on industrial, market, economical and political trends, their use being affected by all such trends at various periods since coal was exported from these shores. Latterly of course they have been taken down and done away with and a new kind of coal handling installation has taken their place - the import quay - where even larger ships than those that ever used these staiths bring millions of tons of coal from half way around the world to feed the power station boilers of a country built on coal.

A final look at North Blyth in the July of 1967. J27 No.65885 prepared and ready for its last journey to the local scrapyard. Condemned on 7th June, the engine is awaiting the buyer which would come along during August and seal its fate once and for all. One of the ten LNER built J27's, this engine emerged from Darlington in June 1923 and went to York shed for a twenty year stint. In March 1943 wartime measures saw it allocated to Neville Hill but it was back at York in February 1950. just over four years later it moved to Selby and then at the end of July 1959 reallocation to Malton had it working from there until September 1960 when it returned once again to York. One year later, exactly, it ventured to Sunderland and had a five year period there. In November 1966 it was allocated to North Blyth. In what should have been its final operational move, it was reallocated (on paper) to Sunderland on 7th May 1967 but as we can see here, it never did leave North Blyth. A last glance at the engine shed reveals the corrugated screens covering openings in the east wall of the roundhouse. These screens had been there since the shed was built and would have originally been constructed of wood. The purpose of the screens was purely temporary, at least in the eyes of the NER planners, for they covered openings in the wall which would have allowed access from this roundhouse into another roundhouse which would have been built alongside but offset further to the north and east on the open ground seen here. The J27's front buffers would have been virtually facing the turntable of the planned shed. However, as can be seen the second shed was never built. Perhaps traffic did not come up to the levels expected or maybe the NER people had been cautiously optimistic and had made reservation - just in case.